Woven cloth is a common and familiar material of the modern world, with a multitude of uses from clothing to furnishings. Nowadays most of the world's cloth is produced industrially not only in the long established manufacturing countries of the Western world, but increasingly in countries which have only recently acquired industrial technology from the West. However, in many parts of the world, even including the British Isles, cloth is still woven by hand on simple looms, by techniques which may have changed little in hundreds or even thousands of years. This handwoven cloth is admired, not least in the industrialised West, for its quality and its distinctive local designs. These can best be appreciated by understanding some of the basic techniques of weaving.

Woven cloth is only one of many materials suitable to the purposes for which it is used. Dressed hide and leather, plaited matting, netting or modern plastic sheet can serve many of the same purposes, often with better effect. Nor can cloth be produced only by weaving. Felt, of wool, hair, or treebark (*barkcloth*) has been used by many peoples around the world. Knitting and lacemaking are completely different from weaving, and industrial technology has devised yet other ways of making unwoven cloth. Weaving, whether on simple hand looms or in industrial factories, is a distinctive technique involving two sets of threads, one, the *warps*, being set up so that the other, the *wefts*, can be passed at right angles alternately over and under them to form the cloth. A loom is a device for stretching the warp threads tight. This enables more efficient weaving techniques to be used, but it is possible to weave without a loom.

Weaving is a very ancient craft, although it is difficult to judge exactly how ancient. By 6000 BC, and possibly earlier, the ancient farming communities of the Near East were making cloth in this way. In Egypt linen cloth has been found which dates to 4000–5000 BC. Although weaving may have spread from these areas to many parts of Asia, Europe and Africa, it was also invented in other places and times. On the other hand many peoples around the world never adopted weaving but devised other ways of making any material they might need. Some of the stages through which weaving may have developed from its simplest beginnings are suggested by methods in use today, or in recent times. These reveal how fine and beautiful cloth can be skilfully made with even the most elementary tools and techniques.

Twining and Finger Weaving

The simplest forms of weaving are similar to basket work except that they require softer, flexible fibres. In some cases it is possible to see how certain peoples developed cloth by adapting basketry techniques to new raw materials. When, as in basket making, the wefts are passed between individual warps with the fingers, the process is known as *finger weaving*.

In New Zealand the Maoris wove cloaks and kilts by a technique very similar to that which they and other Polynesian peoples used to make basketry objects. The material they used was the leaves of a local plant,

known as flax, which could be soaked and beaten to soften and free the strong fibres. The fibres were often joined together and strengthened by twisting them into string or thread. This was done by rubbing them against the thigh with the palm of the hand, but in many cases the fibres were used untwisted and loose. Maori weavers used a technique known at *twining*, in which a pair of weft threads are passed in and out between the warps, taking a half turn around one another between each warp. This anchors the wefts firmly to the warps so that they do not slip. When setting the warp threads up for weaving they were held securely by the first pair of wefts, which were stretched between two sticks set in the ground. The warps hung downwards and the weaving proceeded from top to bottom. The Maoris used many variations of twining to produce different types of cloak. Generally the wefts were widely spaced. For finer cloaks two pairs of wefts were used simultaneously, and ornamental tags or feathers to cover the outside of the cloak could be attached under the wefts as the twining proceeded. For the borders of some cloaks two, three or more wefts were used at once, each dyed a different colour. The weaver

A Maori girl in the last century, wearing a cloak ornamented with tags of thread.

could select which colour appeared at the front of the material to form geometric patterns.

In societies like that of the Maori where people live in small independent communities, individuals are seldom able to make a living solely from crafts. Among the Maori weaving was a woman's occupation. Although some women were better weavers than others, they all wove from time to time to provide their families with clothing and with fine cloaks to give as gifts on ceremonial occasions.

American Indians on the coasts of British Columbia also made garments by twining. Using shredded cedar bark they produced rough cloaks for everyday wear rather similar to those of the Maori, twining wefts of twisted cedar bark string around untwisted warps. These people also made very fine basketry by a similar technique. Fine and valuable cloaks ('Chilkat blankets') were also made to be worn by the high ranking leaders of the community on ceremonial occasions, to proclaim their wealth and prestige. These were made with wefts of white hair or wool from dogs and mountain sheep, twisted into a coarse yarn. When weaving

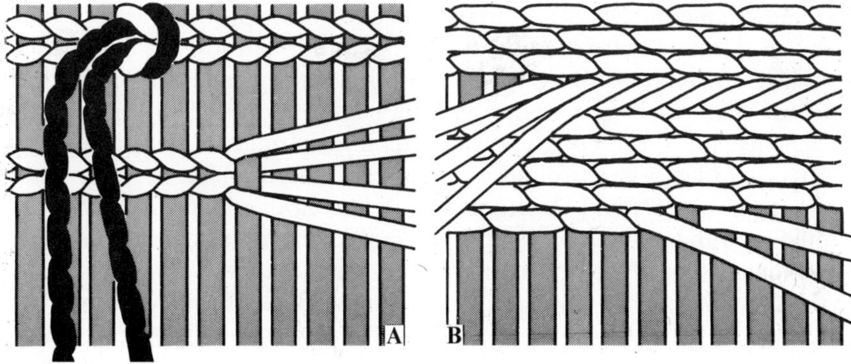

Twining
(a) A Maori technique, using two pairs of wefts simultaneously, showing how ornamental tags were attached.
(b) A technique used on 'Chilkat blankets'. Large areas were woven with a pair of wefts twining around two warps at a time. Twining with three wefts was used for the borders of designs.

(*Left*) Weaving a Chilkat blanket in the last century. The blanket, which is almost finished, is wound around the wooden beam. To keep it clean the material is wrapped and covered, and the loose warps are gathered in small bags. The woman works from a painted pattern board behind the weaving frame. A finished blanket hangs on the wall above.

(*Right*) A Chilkat blanket, woven about 1890.

(*Right*) A Salish weaver, painted in the 1850s. In the background a woman is using the characteristic Salish spindle, plying thread from the ball on the floor, which is twisted together and wound up on the spindle. (*See page 6.*) The thread includes fur from dogs like the one in the foreground.

these Indians suspended the warp threads from a horizontal wooden beam. The weaving proceeded downwards and the finished cloth was wound up around the beam. Twining, by covering both sides of each warp thread with the wefts produces a *weft faced* fabric in which only the wefts show on the surface of the cloth. On the fine woollen cloaks, different sections were woven separately with wefts dyed yellow, black or blue-green, to form elaborate designs. The style of these designs was similar to that of the painting and woodcarving so highly developed by these people. As among the Maori, weaving was a woman's craft, while sculpture was done by men.

The Salish Indians on the coast further south improved on this weaving technique by using a frame with two horizontal beams to weave their finer woollen blankets or cloaks. They used a continuous length of thread wound around the two beams to form a series of warps which were held in tension, forming a true loom. By slackening the tension the area being worked on could be moved around into a convenient position for the weaver. The resulting cylinder of cloth could be opened by cutting the warps leaving the loose ends as a decorative fringe. Alternatively the warp could be passed around a rod or cord and doubled back on itself with each turn around the frame. When the cloth was finished the rod could be withdrawn to leave a flat piece of cloth with no loose ends.

Geometric patterns and designs were produced by twining, working each coloured section separately, as on the 'Chilkat blankets'. However, the tension of the warps on this type of frame was sufficient to hold the

wefts in place without twining them around one another to anchor them to the warps, as was necessary if the warps hung slack. Besides twining the Salish also used the more usual technique of weaving in which the wefts pass alternately over and under the warps without twisting around one another. The simplest method, when the weft passes over and under one warp at a time, produces a *plain weave*. Whether the warps or the wefts form the face of the cloth with this technique depends on various things, such as their thickness in relation to one another, and how many of each there are to the centimetre. The Salish blankets were weft faced. By weaving single wefts over and under several warps at a time in a regular sequence (*twilled weave*) they created repetitive patterns such as herringbone.

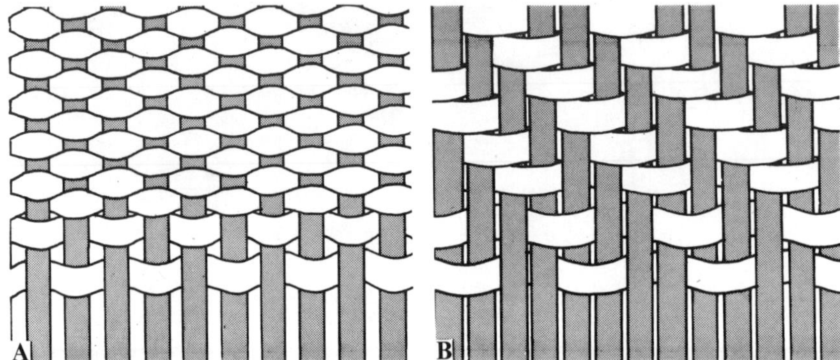

(a) Plain weave.
(b) Twilled weave.

The Salish improved the quality of their thread by spinning it with a *spindle*, a stick with a wooden flywheel or *whorl* which was revolved in the hands. Variations of this technique are widespread around the world. Often the spindle is suspended from a hank of fibre which is drawn out, pulled taut by the weight of the spindle and twisted as the spindle revolves. By repeating the process, with thread instead of loose fibre, several strands may be *plied* into one strong thread. (*See inside back cover and page 5.*)

Weaving with Shed Stick and Heddle

Although twining and finger weaving can produce beautiful cloths, as the work of the Maori and the Northwest Coast Indians shows, it is a slow and exacting process, requiring more time and labour than many other weaving techniques. Greater speed can be obtained if all the warp threads which a weft must pass before or behind can be separated simultaneously into two sets, to form an opening or *shed* the full width of the cloth. A basic method of forming sheds is shown in the diagram. The warps are separated into two sets of alternate threads by a *shed stick*. This allows the weft to be passed quickly in one direction, passing over and under the same warps as the shed stick. When the weft is passed back in the opposite direction the position of the warps has to be reversed so that those previously in front of the weft are behind, and vice versa. To allow for this the

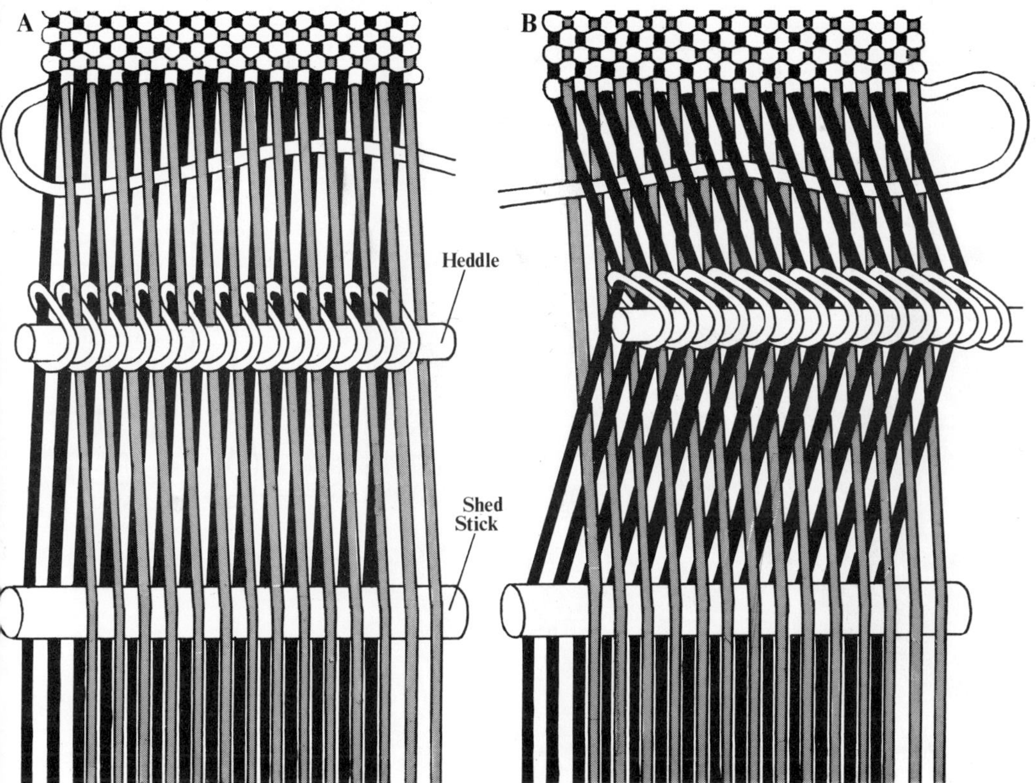

warps hanging behind the shed stick are attached by loops of thread (*leashes*) to another stick. This enables them to be pulled forward to form a second shed (a *counter shed*) in front of the other set. This device (known as a *heddle*) is placed between the shed stick and the finished cloth. Because they are in tension the second set of warps may return automatically to their original positions. On the other hand they may have to be forced back with a stick or with the fingers, because of the friction between the two sets of warps where they cross one another.

A loom set up with the simple arrangement of shed stick and heddle shown in this diagram produces a plain weave. Many types of loom around the world are operated in basically the same way, though they may also be designed to produce more elaborate weaves. According to the arrangement of the warps they may be vertical, as in the diagram, or horizontal. A simple example of a vertical loom is shown on ancient Greek vase paintings of the 6th and 5th centuries BC. On these looms the warps hung from an overhead beam around which the finished cloth could be wound. The warps were kept taut by hanging weights, a method which may have been used by the earliest weavers of the Near East and Egypt.

In parts of Nigeria women weave cotton cloth on a simple vertical loom, which, like the Salish loom, has a continuous length of warp thread wound around two beams so that a cylinder of cloth is produced. This loom is rather more complicated than the warp weighted loom, although it works

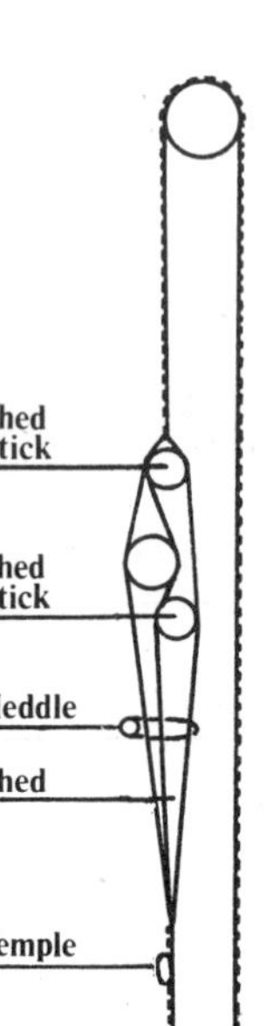

A Nigerian woman weaving. She is pulling the heddle and widening the resulting shed by inserting the beater. The weft is wound on a long spool which leans against the loom to the right. The diagram shows the loom in cross section, with the shed formed by the shed sticks.

on the same principle. The weaver works from the bottom of the loom upwards. Besides the heddle there are two shed sticks and a third stick inserted into the threads held forward by the shed sticks. Like a shed stick, this helps to keep the warps evenly spaced and to increase their tension. Forming sheds allows each new weft to be forced against the one before across the full width of the cloth, with a *beater*. This West African loom has a flat stick which is inserted into the shed and pulled sharply downwards beating each weft against the one before. Below the edge of the cloth another stick, the *temple* is used to keep the width of the cloth even, since the wefts tend to pull the warps inwards and narrow the cloth. The temple has small spikes on each end which are simply inserted into the edges of the cloth.

In setting up even a simple loom with two beams, rather than weights, great care has to be taken to ensure that all the warp threads are stretched to the same degree, otherwise the resulting cloth will be crinkled and uneven, and some warps may snap by being stretched tighter than the rest. If the warp threads are continuous a way of avoiding this is to wind them carefully around a frame or a series of sticks to arrange them correctly, at even tension, for mounting on the frame of the loom.

Looms similar to the Nigerian example, with a shed stick and heddle, are used over wide areas of West-Central Africa, to weave a rather inflexible cloth from shredded raffia leaf. As the 'threads' are unspun and thus of limited length, the warps and wefts cannot be continuous. Each is a separate thread with loose ends which form a fringe all around the cloth. Other variants of the simple vertical loom are used, for instance, by the Berbers of North Africa, and by the Navaho Indians of the USA.

Horizontal Looms

Looms may also be horizontal, and it is on such looms that the most complex weaving techniques have been developed. A simple form of horizontal loom is used by Bedouin and some peasant women of Arabia and North Africa to weave a coarse woollen or goat's hair cloth for tents and wall hangings, rugs, bags and other domestic articles. The tension of this loom is maintained by stretching the warp between two beams, held in place by pegs in the ground. One set of alternate warps is kept constantly raised by a heddle, supported on stones at a fixed height above the ground. This forms one shed and the other is formed by moving the shed stick and by pulling the lower set of warps by hand to raise them above those held by the heddle. The weft is wound on a stick spool in order to pass it through the shed. It is beaten in firmly with a flat stick, and by pulling down between the warps with a hook. On horizontal looms the weavers work away from themselves, and the Bedouin weavers sit on the finished cloth. The cloth is normally warp faced, and stripes are formed by using different coloured warps. Patterns are also made by twining the wefts which gives a weft faced fabric (*see inside front cover*). This simple loom is well suited to the Bedouins' nomadic way of life. The actual loom is little more than a collection of beams and sticks, and it can easily be rolled into a bundle and packed for transport. Other nomadic peoples of the Middle East, Pakistan and North Africa also use this type of loom. Similar fixed heddle looms are also used in East Africa and Madagascar.

The Bedouin loom.
(a) The shed formed by the heddle, but widened by turning the beater on edge.
(b) The shed formed by raising the warps passing over the shed stick above those held by the heddle.

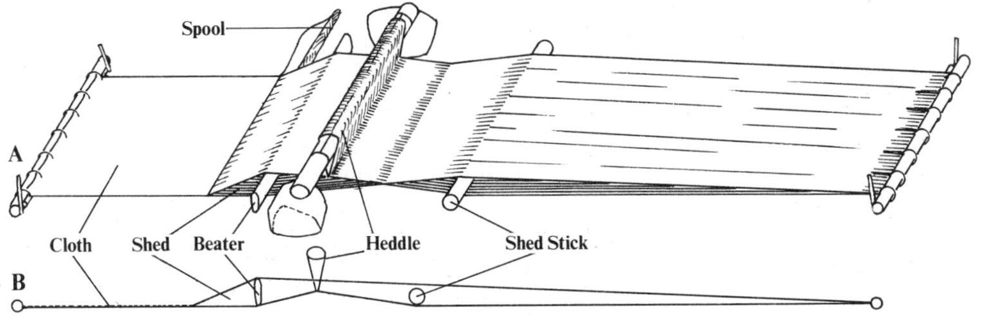

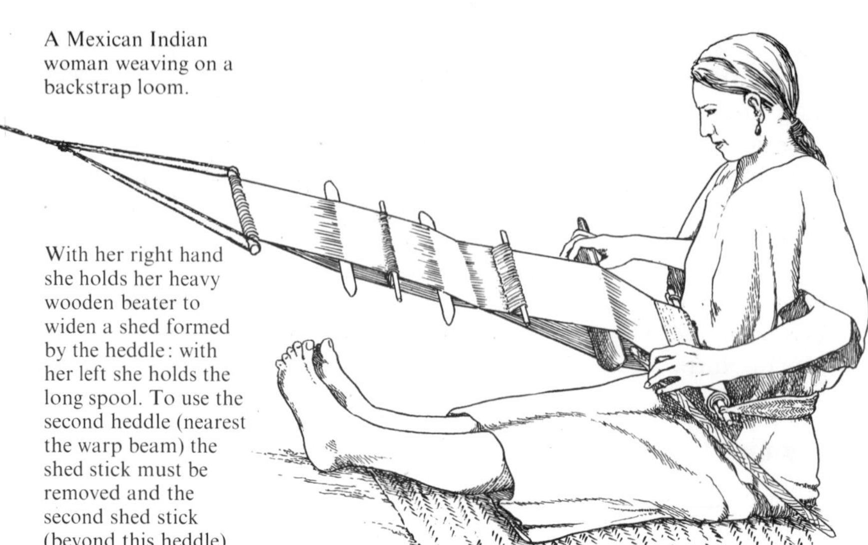

A Mexican Indian woman weaving on a backstrap loom.

With her right hand she holds her heavy wooden beater to widen a shed formed by the heddle: with her left she holds the long spool. To use the second heddle (nearest the warp beam) the shed stick must be removed and the second shed stick (beyond this heddle) comes into use.

Another widespread type of horizontal loom relies on the weight of the weaver's body to stretch the warps during weaving. One end of the warps is attached to a fixed beam or post and the other to a *breast beam* held to the weaver's body by a belt or strap. The weaving proceeds away from the weaver towards the fixed *warp beam*. Like the Bedouin loom, this *backstrap* loom, having no frame, can easily be rolled up when not in use. The backstrap loom is the one most commonly used by the Indians of South America. Many fine and beautifully patterned cloths produced in this way have survived from the ancient civilisations of Peru, mostly in excellently preserved burials. Today, from Mexico to Chile many rural Indian women continue to weave cotton or woollen cloth on backstrap looms for their families' use or for trade in local markets.

This South American loom relies on a shed stick to raise one set of alternate warps, forming the first shed, and a heddle by which the other set can be raised to form the second shed. A beater may be inserted in each shed to open it further as well as to beat in the weft. *Lease* or *laze* rods, threaded through the warps beyond the shed stick help to space the warps and keep them at an even tension. This type of loom allows for an enormouse variety of weaving techniques and the ancient Peruvians in particular made use of almost every type of weave known today. Decorative patterns and motifs can be woven into the cloth in many different ways. If the cloth is to be weft faced, motifs can be produced by weaving different sections separately with different colour wefts (this technique is often known as *tapestry* weaving). The normal wefts passing from side to side of the cloth can alternate with wefts of a different colour which pass over and under a number of wefts at a time, to '*float*' on the upper surface of the finished cloth (*brocade*). For small irregular motifs or patterns the wefts can best be inserted with the fingers or with a needle, using a small stick to form a new shed between the appropriate warps for each weft to

pass through. Repetitive patterns can be created more efficiently by using several heddles so that the warps can be raised in a number of different combinations in a regular sequence (*see front and back covers*).

Backstrap looms are also used in India and in many parts of Southeast Asia, from Assam and Burma to Indonesia, in some of the Pacific islands of Melanesia, and by the Ainu, an indigenous people of Japan. The advantage of these looms is that they are portable and easy to dismantle and store away. They are used especially by people in tribal or peasant communities who weave to supply cloth for their families, or perhaps to sell locally as a supplement to their other income. In Indonesia the weaving of decorative cloths of cotton and silk on backstrap looms is especially highly developed for making the finest ceremonial clothing. Besides brocading, one highly developed technique is to dye the warp threads and sometimes the wefts as well before weaving, to form patterns (*Ikat*).

Treadle Looms

On all the looms described so far the sheds are formed by hand, which in some cases involves considerably delay between the insertion of each weft. In many parts of the world looms are fitted with treadles so that the sheds can be formed by the action of the feet, leaving the hands free to ply the weft with greater speed. A simple treadle mechanism is used on a type of loom widespread in West Africa. Unlike the broad upright looms used by women in this area, this horizontal loom is used exclusively by men, to weave narrow strips of cotton cloth. This loom has a pair of heddles, one to raise the even warps and the other the odd, so that a shed stick is not required. Each heddle is strung between a pair of rods (*shafts*) so that it can be pulled down as well as up, and the lower rods are attached by cords to a pair of simple treadles. The heddles are joined by

11

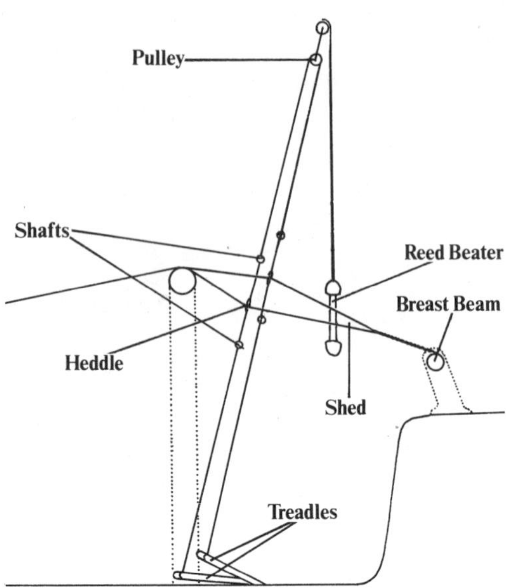

another cord which runs through a pulley above the loom so that as one heddle is pulled down it pulls the other up. The weft is wound on a spool fitted inside a wooden casing or *shuttle* which allows it to slide easily through the shed. Instead of a simple stick beater the tool for beating in the weft is a wooden frame set with vertical strips of reed, which pass between each warp. This also helps to space the warps and prevent them tangling. On this loom simple designs are often produced by using warps or wefts of different colours, producing stripes the length or breadth of the cloth. Tapestry or brocaded patterns may be inserted by hand or by using additional heddles. Larger scale patterns are formed when the narrow strips of cloth are sewn together to make clothing.

In the simplest form of this West African loom, used in Sierra Leone, the heddle pulley is suspended from a simple tripod of sticks which is moved along the stretched out warps as the weaving progresses. In other parts, however, a more elaborate four post frame is used, supporting a breast beam around which the finished cloth is wound and a second, higher beam beyond the heddles over which the warps pass to keep them taut and at a convenient angle. The reed beater is suspended from the frame so that it can be swung against the wefts. The warps are separate threads and their far ends are fixed to a peg or to stones, which can be moved as the finished cloth is wound up.

There are many ways to construct horizontal treadle looms of this basic type. In most cases the warps on these looms are fixed at both ends, but in Japan and parts of Southeast Asia treadles are fitted to backstrap looms, on the frame which supports the warp beam of backstrap looms in this part of the world. However, there is a limit to the size of loom which

A Nigerian treadle loom. The heddles and reed beater are suspended from a horizontal rod above the weaver's head. The diagram shows a cross section of the loom.

can be stretched by a backstrap and larger looms for broad pieces of cloth require fixed beams to stretch the warps. Such looms may be constructed with freestanding frames to hold the beams and heddle mechanisms, or built into a permanent workshop. Posts may be sunk into the floor to support the warps, and the heddles may be suspended from the ceiling or from a separate beam. On one type of Indian loom the warps are at ground level and the treadle mechanism is in a pit on the edge of which the weaver sits. The warps are individual threads, not one continuous length, which allows cloth to be woven in very long strips. They are commonly wound around the warp beam, to be unwound as the weaving progresses and the cloth is taken up around the breast beam. This necessitates a way of fixing the beams which will prevent them from unwinding with the tension of the warps. In South-East Asia a flat board, held in slots, is used as a warp beam and this is turned over once each time a new length of warp is to be released. On other looms, such as those used by some Arab weavers, the warps are stretched over beams above the loom and fixed to a weight or peg in the wall behind the weaver's back. As the warps are used up, new lengths can be added to the ends. This avoids repeated warping up and the threading of new warps through the heddles each time one set of warps is used up. The breast beam is fixed by a common technique; a rod, inserted through a hole in the end of the beam, one end of which rests against the floor or some solid fixture on the loom. On many treadle looms heddles may be joined, not by a single cord passing through a pulley but by a cord from each heddle tied to opposite ends of a short stick. This *heddle-raiser* is itself suspended from its centre by another cord and as a treadle pulls one heddle downwards it tilts and lifts the other heddle up.

Treadle looms have been most highly developed in societies where people make their living by different occupations, crafts and trades, exchanging and selling their produce with one another. The more complex treadle looms, being more efficient, are a valuable investment for those who make their living by weaving. In many societies the expense of constructing such a loom and perhaps building a permanent workshop is prohibitive, so simple portable looms may be more suitable for casual weavers who make cloth for their own families but get their living in other ways. In other cases professional weavers have also relied upon these simple looms. In Peru under the Inca empire, full time weavers worked on backstrap looms and today some Indian peasants of South America supplement their income by selling cloth in local markets. On the other hand quite complex treadle looms have been used by domestic weavers in societies where wealth and technological skill enabled them to be constructed with relatively little expense.

To supply the quantity of thread needed for professional weaving on large and efficient looms the speed of spinning has been increased by the use of a spinning wheel. The large flywheel serves the same purpose as the whorl on a simple spindle, but, when spun, it turns a separate spindle by means of a cord running around the two. In its simplest form the wheel is

turned by hand, as today in India where the spinning wheel may have originated. Such wheels were also used throughout Europe until a treadle action was added in the sixteenth century, and in some districts they survived into quite recent times. Chinese spinning wheels also have treadles, and the wheel may turn several spindles at once. Professional weavers often rely on spinners to supply them with thread rather than make it themselves. Other specialists make a living from dyeing the thread or finished cloth, and it may be sold by merchants. Often different craftsmen and tradesmen form associations to regulate their trade, like the guilds of medieval Europe.

Complex Looms

It was in societies where weaving and other crafts became specialised professions that more complex looms were developed, to increase the efficiency of weaving and to produce specialised types of cloth. Thus for instance the basic two-treadle loom was modified to speed the production of complex weaves and patterned fabrics by an increase in the number of foot-operated heddles. This facilitates the weaving of complex patterns without the need for selecting odd warps by hand. In India this technique is used to produce a variety of finely patterned cloths. There is a limit to the number of heddles which can conveniently be operated by foot treadles alone and the invention of the *draw loom*, used for weaving silk in com-

plex designs, enabled a greater variety of sheds to be formed. Instead of heddles the warps were raised by cords which ran to each warp in the set required to form a particular shed. The cords from each warp in a set joined a single cord which passed up over the loom. An assistant pulled each of these numerous cords as required to form the different sheds, while the weaver plied the shuttle. Foot-operated heddles were also used to form the standard weave with which the wefts forming the patterns were interspersed for strength. Such looms, developed in Asia, were used by commercial weavers in Europe from the Middle Ages until the industrial revolution to produce richly patterned cloths. The horizontal treadle loom continued to be used for domestic weaving and for the commercial production of simple fabrics. It is still used, for instance, by the hand-loom weavers of the Hebrides. Although the development of large and complex looms improved the regularity of the weave, their main advantage was to speed the production of cloth. As we have seen, fine cloth and elaborate woven designs can be produced on even the simplest looms, although the work is slow and painstaking by comparison with more mechanised hand looms.

During the industrial revolution of the eighteenth and nineteenth centuries mechanical weaving devices were invented to propel the shuttle and select the sheds automatically, and water and steam were used to power the looms. The basic techniques of weaving remain the same as they have been for centuries, even to this day. The advantage of modern power looms, to their owners at least, is that they weave extremely rapidly and require very little skilled labour compared to hand looms. For this reason the hand-loom weavers of England suffered drastic unemployment during the industrial revolution, and in modern times traditional weavers face similar problems in various parts of the world. With industrialisation Britain and other countries began to export large quantities of cloth to the colonies of Africa and Asia. The cloth, often printed in local designs to appeal to traditional tastes, supplanted local or imported handwoven cloth for many purposes in many areas.

In this century many non-Western countries have established their own textile and clothing industries. Local crafts inevitably suffer from competition with mass-produced goods, as well as from the changes of fashion resulting from colonialism and international trade. Today cheap manufactured clothing of Western style has become the everyday clothing of many peoples who until recently wore handwoven cloth. This cloth is now often used only for best traditional dress. Local craftsmen in some areas now produce traditional cloth mainly for Western tourists or collectors who can pay prices beyond the means of local people. However, hand-loom weaving cannot be sustained by a fashionable Western interest in local craftsmanship. Today the economic forces of industrialisation and international commerce are inevitably destroying hand-loom weaving in many countries where it once flourished, a process which began two hundred years ago in Britain.

Further Reading

A good basic introduction to weaving is Leslie J. Clarke: *The Craftsman in Textiles* (G. Bell & Sons 1968)

Useful studies of particular weaving traditions include:

Shelagh Weir: *Spinning and Weaving in Palestine* (British Museum, 1970)

Venice Lamb: *West African Weaving* (Duckworth 1975)

Gladys Reichart: *Weaving a Navajo Blanket* (Dover 1974)

Barbara Taber & Marilyn Anderson: *Backstrap Weaving* (Pitman 1975)

Other books may be consulted at the Museum of Mankind.

(*Right*)
Spinning with a simple spindle. This Bedouin woman holds a hank of loose wool in her left hand and teases it into thread, which is twisted by the revolving spindle.

(*Back cover*)
Tapestry with a pattern of monkeys, from a Peruvian grave about 1000 years old. (*See page 10.*)

© 1977 The Trustees of the British Museum

Published by British Museum Publications Limited, 6 Bedford Square, London WC1B 3RA

Designed by James Shurmer

Photographs appear by courtesy of the following:
S. Weir, inside front cover, page 14 (bottom), inside back cover; Royal Ontario Museum, page 5 (bottom); J. Picton, pages 8, 12. All others, Museum of Mankind. Drawings and diagrams by Ben Burt.

ISBN 0 7141 0070 6

Printed in England by Martin Cadbury, Worcester